Born in 1974

by

Kerry Butters.

Born in 1974

Millennium: 2nd millennium

Centuries: 19th century – **20th century** – 21st century

Decades: 1940s 1950s 1960s – **1970s** – 1980s 1990s 2000s

Years: 1971 1972 1973 – **1974** – 1975 1976 1977

1974 (MCMLXXIV) was a common year starting on Tuesday (dominical letter F) of the Gregorian calendar, the 1974th year of the Common Era (CE) and *Anno Domini* (AD) designations, the 974th year of the 2nd millennium, the 74th year of the 20th century, and the 5th year of the 1970s decade.

Contents

- 1 Events
- 2 Births
- 3 Deaths
- 4 Nobel Prizes
- 5 In the News

Events

January

- January 20 – The General Dynamics F-16 Fighting Falcon makes its first flight at Edwards Air Force Base, California.
- January 26 – Bülent Ecevit, of CHP forms the new government of Turkey (37th government, partner MSP).

February

- February 1
  - Fire breaks out in the Joelma Building in São Paulo, Brazil; 177 die, 293 are injured, 11 die later of their injuries.
  - Kuala Lumpur, the capital of Malaysia, is declared a Federal Territory.
- February 4
  - Heiress Patty Hearst, is kidnapped outside her Berkeley, California apartment by the Symbionese Liberation Army.
- February 8 – After a record 84 days in orbit, the crew of *Skylab 4* returns to Earth.
- February 17 – A soccer stampede occurs in Cairo, killing 49.

March

- March 3 – Turkish Airlines Flight 981 travelling from Paris to London crashes in a wood near Paris, killing all 346 aboard.

- March 4
  - Following a hung parliament in the United Kingdom general election, Conservative prime minister Edward Heath resigns and is succeeded by Labour's Harold Wilson, who previously led the country from 1964 to 1970.
  - *People* magazine's first issue released in the U.S. with Mia Farrow on the cover.
- March 8
  - Charles de Gaulle Airport opens in Paris, France;
  - Queen releases Queen II with the single Seven Seas of Rhye, starting their legendary canon of hit singles.
- March 10 – Japanese holdout: A Japanese World War II soldier, Second Lieutenant Hiroo Onoda, surrenders in the Philippines.
- March 18
  - End of 1973 oil crisis: Most OPEC nations end a 5-month oil embargo against the United States, Europe and Japan.
  - After 23 consecutive years on television, Lucille Ball airs the series finale of *Here's Lucy* and does not continue a weekly television series.
- March 29
  - The Terracotta Army of Qin Shi Huang is discovered at Xi'an, China.
  - Launch of the Volkswagen Golf in West Germany, a modern front-wheel drive hatchback which is expected to replace the iconic Volkswagen Beetle, holder of the world record for the car with the most units produced.

April

April – The world population reaches 4 billion people estimated by the United States Census Bureau.

- April 2 – French president Georges Pompidou, dies of cancer at 63. Alain Poher succeeds him immediately; Valéry Giscard d'Estaing wins the presidential contest in May 1974.
- April 3–4 – An enormous tornado outbreak strikes the central parts of the United States, killing around 319 people. Known as the

"1974 Super Outbreak", the event was the largest of its kind until the 2011 Super Outbreak.

- April 4 – Hank Aaron ties Babe Ruth for the all-time home run record with his 714th at Riverfront Stadium in Cincinnati.
- April 5 – Stephen King publishes *Carrie*, his first novel.
- April 6
  - Swedish pop group ABBA's song "Waterloo" wins the 1974 Eurovision Song Contest in Brighton, England, UK.
  - California Jam is held at the Ontario Motor Speedway in Ontario, California, attracting 250,000 fans.
- April 8 – Hank Aaron became the all-time MLB home run leader with his 715th at Atlanta in front of a national television audience.
- April 11 – The Kiryat Shmona massacre takes place in Israel.
- April 15 – As "Tania", Patty Hearst is photographed wielding an M1 carbine while robbing the Sunset District branch of the Hibernia Bank in San Francisco.
- April 24 – *Guillaume Affair*: exposure of an East German spy Günter Guillaume within the West German government, leading to the resignation of West German Chancellor Willy Brandt.
- April 25 – *Carnation Revolution*: A right-wing military coup in Portugal restores democracy, ending 48 years of Estado Novo and Ditadura Nacional dictatorship in the country. Portuguese Prime Minister Marcelo Caetano flees to Brazil and is granted political asylum by Brazilian President Ernesto Geisel.

May

- May 4
  - An all-female Japanese team summits Manaslu in Nepal, becoming the first women to climb an 8,000 metre peak.
  - The Expo '74 world's fair opens in Spokane, Washington.
- May 6 - Willy Brandt West Germany's chancellor resigns; replaced by Helmut Schmidt
- May 17 – Dublin and Monaghan bombings: The Ulster Volunteer Force (UVF), explode four car bombs in Dublin and Monaghan in the Republic of Ireland. The attacks kill 33 civilians and wound

almost 300, the highest number of casualties in any single day during "The Troubles".

- A massive, two-hour shootout between the Los Angeles Police Department and members of the Symbionese Liberation Army leaves six SLA members, including SLA leader Donald DeFreeze, dead.
- May 18
  - Nuclear test: Under Project Smiling Buddha, India successfully detonates its first nuclear weapon, becoming the 6th nation to do so.
  - The Warsaw radio mast is completed, the second tallest structure ever built (it collapses on August 8, 1991).
- May 19 – The Philadelphia Flyers defeat the Boston Bruins to become the first team from the 1967 NHL expansion class to win the Stanley Cup in the North American National Hockey League.
- May 30 – NASA's ATS-6 satellite is launched.

June

- June 4 – The Cleveland Indians stage an ill-advised Ten Cent Beer Night for a game against the Texas Rangers at Cleveland Municipal Stadium. Cleveland forfeits after alcohol-fueled mayhem and violence spreads from the stands onto the field.
- June 13 – The 1974 FIFA World Cup begins in West Germany.
- June 26 – The Universal Product Code is scanned for the first time, to sell a package of Wrigley's chewing gum at the Marsh Supermarket in Troy, Ohio.
- June 29
  - Isabel Perón is sworn in as the first female President of Argentina, replacing her sick husband Juan Perón, who dies 2 days later.
  - America Sings attraction opens to the public for the first time at Disneyland in Anaheim, California.

July

- July 7 – West Germany beats the Netherlands 2–1 to win the 1974 FIFA World Cup. The West German football team are awarded the new FIFA World Cup Trophy.
- July 8 – Two weeks after the attraction's opening, an 18-year-old employee is crushed to her death while working on America Sings at Disneyland. This is the first casualty to occur to an employee at a Disney Park.
- July 15 – News anchor Christine Chubbuck commits suicide during a live broadcast on WXLT-TV in Sarasota, Florida.
- July 19 – Railcar explosion in Decatur, Illinois. A tanker car collides with a Norfolk & Western boxcar. Seven people are killed, 349 are injured and $18 million in property damage.
- July 20 – The Turkish invasion of Cyprus occurs.
- July 23 – The Greek military junta is replaced by a civilian government in Greece concluding the seven-year military rule.

August

38th US President Gerald R. Ford

- August 4 – A bomb explodes in a train between Italy and West Germany, killing 12 and wounding 48. Italian neo-fascists take responsibility.
- August 7 – Philippe Petit crosses between Twin Towers World Trade Center high-wire walking
- August 8 – Watergate scandal: U.S. President Richard Nixon announces his resignation (effective August 9).
- August 9 – Vice President Gerald Ford succeeds Richard Nixon as the 38th President of the United States, upon Nixon's resignation.

- August 14 – Turkey invades Cyprus for the second time, occupying 37% of the island's territory.
- August 30 – An express train bound for Germany from Belgrade derails in Zagreb, Yugoslavia (now Croatia), killing more than 150 passengers.

September

- September 8
  - TWA Flight 841 crashes into the Ionian Sea 18 minutes after take off from Athens, after a bomb explodes in the cargo hold, and kills 88 people.
  - President Gerald Ford pardons former president Richard Nixon.
- September 10 – The Portuguese military junta grants independence to Guinea-Bissau.
- September 12 – Emperor Haile Selassie of Ethiopia is deposed by the Derg, bringing an end to the Solomonic dynasty's rule since 1270. The Ethiopian Civil War begins.
- September 13 – Japanese Red Army members seize the French Embassy in The Hague, Netherlands.
- September 20 – The Kootenai War is declared, and 10-cent tolls are charged on U.S. Highway 95.
- September 23 – Ceefax (one of the first public service information systems) is started by the BBC.

October

- October 11 – The UK Labour government of Harold Wilson wins the second general election of the year, forming a three-seat majority. Wilson, who has led the party for a total of 11 years, has now won four of the five general elections he has contested.
- October 30 – The Rumble in the Jungle takes place in Kinshasa, Zaire, where Muhammad Ali knocks out George Foreman in 8 rounds to regain the Heavyweight title, which had been stripped from him 7 years earlier.

November

- November 1
  - The World Tourism Organization (WTO or WToO) is established.
  - The German electronic band Kraftwerk releases their studio album *Autobahn*.
- November 13 – Ronald DeFeo, Jr., murders his entire family in their home in Amityville on Long Island, an event that inspires the story of *The Amityville Horror*.
- November 16 – Arecibo message: The radio telescope at the Arecibo Observatory on Puerto Rico sends an interstellar radio message towards Messier 13, the Great Globular Cluster in Hercules. The message will reach its destination around the year 27,000.
- November 21 – Birmingham pub bombings: In Birmingham, England, two pubs are bombed, killing 21 people in an attack widely believed at the time to be linked to the Provisional Irish Republican Army. The Birmingham Six are later sentenced to life in prison for this, but their convictions are quashed after a lengthy campaign.
- November 18 – The International Energy Agency is founded.
- November 22 – The United Nations General Assembly grants the Palestine Liberation Organization observer status.
- November 24 – A skeleton from the hominid species *Australopithecus afarensis* is discovered and named Lucy.
- November 26 – Anneline Kriel is crowned as Miss World 1974, the second South African to hold the title after Penny Coelen in 1958, when Helen Morgan resigns four days after winning the 24th Miss World pageant.
- November 28 – In a rare public performance, former Beatle John Lennon joins Elton John on stage at Madison Square Garden in New York City.

December

- December 1 – A Boeing 727 carrying TWA Flight 514 crashes 25 miles (40 km) northwest of Dulles International Airport during bad weather, killing all 92 people on board.
- December 9 – The Paris summit, reuniting the European Communities' heads of state and government, commences.
- December 13 – Malta becomes a republic.
- December 17 – The World Intellectual Property Organization (WIPO) becomes a specialized agency of the United Nations.
- December 24–25 – Darwin, Australia is almost completely destroyed by Cyclone Tracy.
- December 30 – Japanese holdout: The last Japanese World War II soldier, Taiwan-born Private Teruo Nakamura, surrenders on the Indonesian island of Morota, 34 years after beginning service in the Imperial Japanese Army.

Date unknown

- Rubik's Cube puzzle is invented by Hungarian architecture professor Ernő Rubik.
- *Dungeons & Dragons* fantasy tabletop role-playing game, designed by Gary Gygax and Dave Arneson, is first released, in the United States.
- PepsiCo becomes the first American company to sell products in the Soviet Union.

Births

January

Ed Helms

Christian Bale

- January 1 – Reem Maged, Egyptian journalist
- January 3 – Alessandro Petacchi, Italian professional road cyclist
- January 10 – Hrithik Roshan, Bollywood actor
- January 12
  - Melanie Chisholm, English singer-songwriter (Spice Girls)
  - Tor Arne Hetland, Norwegian cross-country skier
- January 16 – Kate Moss, English model

- January 17 – Danny Bhoy, Scottish stand-up comedian
- January 18 – Maulik Pancholy, American actor
- January 18 – Gustavo Kupinski, Argentine guitarist (d. 2011)
- January 19 – Éva Novodomszky, Hungarian journalist and presenter
- January 20 – Rae Carruth, former NFL wide receiver
- January 22 – Joseph Muscat, 13th Prime Minister of Malta
- January 23 – Tiffani Thiessen, American actress
- January 24 – Ed Helms, American actor and stand-up comedian
- January 27 – Ole Einar Bjørndalen, Norwegian biathlete
- January 28 – Kari Traa, Norwegian freestyle skier
- January 29
    - Kōji Wada, Japanese rock singer (d. 2016)
    - Michael Andersen, Danish basketball player
- January 30
    - Christian Bale, English actor
    - Olivia Colman, English actress

February

Seth Green

Elizabeth Banks

Jerry O'Connell

James Blunt

- February 4 – Urmila Matondkar, Indian actress
- February 6 – Aljo Bendijo, Filipino journalist, broadcaster, TV/radio host
- February 7
  - Cheryl Cosim, Filipino journalist, news anchor, TV host

- o J Dilla, also known as Jay-Dee, African-American hip-hop producer (d. 2006)
- o Steve Nash, Canadian basketball player
- o Jun Seba, also known as Nujabes, Japanese hip-hop producer (d. 2010)
- February 8
  - o Seth Green, American actor
  - o Guy-Manuel de Homem-Christo, French musician and record producer (Daft Punk)
  - o Kimbo Slice, Bahamian-born American boxer and mixed martial artist (d. 2016)
- February 10
  - o Elizabeth Banks, American actress
  - o Ivri Lider, Israeli singer
- February 13 – Robbie Williams, English rock singer
- February 14
  - o Philippe Léonard, Belgian footballer
  - o Valentina Vezzali, Italian fencer
- February 15
  - o Miranda July, American author, director, actor, musician and spoken-word artist
  - o Mr Lordi, Finnish rock singer (*Lordi*)
  - o Alexander Wurz, Austrian racing driver
- February 17 – Jerry O'Connell, American actor
- February 18 - Jillian Michaels, American personal trainer, businesswoman, author and TV personality
- February 22 – James Blunt, English singer
- February 24
  - o Chad Hugo, American rock musician and producer
  - o Bonnie Somerville, American actress
- February 26 – Sébastien Loeb, French rally driver
- February 27 – Hiroyasu Shimizu, Japanese speed skater

March

Eva Mendes

Ted Kravitz

Alyson Hannigan

- March 1 – Mark-Paul Gosselaar, American actor
- March 3 – David Faustino, American actor
-

- March 4
  - Karol Kučera, Slovakian tennis player
  - Ariel Ortega, Argentine football player
- March 5
  - Jens Jeremies, German footballer
  - Matt Lucas, British comedian
  - Eva Mendes, American actress
  - Barbara Schöneberger, German actress, singer, and TV host
  - Hiten Tejwani, Indian model and actor
- March 6
  - Anthony Carelli, Canadian professional wrestler
  - Cooper Manning, television host, brother of football players Peyton and Eli Manning
- March 7
  - Jenna Fischer, American actress
  - Antonio de la Rúa, Argentine lawyer
- March 12 – Hekiru Shiina, Japanese voice actress and J-pop singer
- March 14 – Grace Park, American born Canadian actress
- March 15 – Percy Montgomery, South African rugby union player
- March 20 – Carsten Ramelow, German footballer
- March 21 – Ted Kravitz, British presenter and Formula One pit-lane reporter
- March 22
  - Marcus Camby, American basketball player
  - Kidada Jones, American actress
  - Bassem Youssef, Egyptian journalist
- March 24 – Alyson Hannigan, American actress
- March 25 – Lark Voorhies, American actress and singer
- March 28
  - Daisuke Kishio, Japanese voice actor
  - Scott Mills, British radio DJ, television presenter and occasional actor
- March 29 – Miguel Gómez, Colombian photographer
- March 30 – Miho Komatsu, Japanese pop singer and songwriter
- March 31 – Jani Sievinen, Finnisher former swimmer

April

Penélope Cruz

- April 1 – Marcos Balter, Brazilian composer
- April 2 – Håkan Hellström, Swedish musician
- April 9 – Jenna Jameson, American pornographic actress
- April 8 – Chris Kyle, most lethal sniper in American military history (d. 2013)
- April 11
  - Tricia Helfer, Canadian actress and model
  - Alexander Kuoppala, Finnish guitarist (ex-Children of Bodom)
- April 12 – Marley Shelton, American actress
- April 13 – Marta Jandová, Czech musician and actress
- April 15
  - Danny Pino, Cuban American actor
  - Tim Thomas, American ice hockey goaltender
- April 16 – Xu Jinglei, Chinese actress and director
- April 17
  - Mikael Åkerfeldt, Swedish musician (Opeth)
  - Victoria Beckham, English singer (Spice Girls)
- April 18 – Edgar Wright, English film director
- April 20 – Tina Cousins, English singer
- April 21 – Faust, Norwegian drummer
- April 22 – Shavo Odadjian, Armenian-born rock bassist (*System of a Down*)

- April 23 – Barry Watson, American actor
- April 28 – Penélope Cruz, Spanish actress
- April 29 – Anggun, Indonesian-French singer-songwriter

May

Breckin Meyer

Laura Pausini

Steve Cardenas

Kenan Doğulu

- May 1
  - ○ Kellie Crawford, Australian singer and actress (Hi-5 and Teen Queens)
  - ○ Lornah Kiplagat, Kenyan-Dutch runner
- May 2
  - ○ Matt Berry, English actor and singer
  - ○ Horacio Carbonari, Argentinian footballer and manager
  - ○ Garðar Thór Cortes, Icelandic tenor and actor
  - ○ Andy Johnson, English-Welsh footballer
  - ○ Janek Meet, Estonian footballer
- May 3
  - ○ Princess Haya bint Al Hussein of Jordan
  - ○ Peter Everitt, Australian footballer and radio host
- May 4
  - ○ Miguel Cairo, Venezuelan baseball player and coach
  - ○ Tony McCoy, Irish jockey and sportscaster
- May 6
  - ○ Bernard Barmasai, Kenyan runner
  - ○ Daniela Bártová, Czech pole vaulter and gymnast
  - ○ Faruk Namdar, German-Turkish footballer
  - ○ Patrick Tang, Hong Kong actor and singer
- May 7
  - ○ Breckin Meyer, American actor
  - ○ Lawrence Johnson, American pole vaulter
  - ○ Ian Pearce, English footballer and manager
- May 8
  - ○ Marge Kõrkjas, Estonian swimmer

- Korey Stringer, American football player (d. 2001)
  - Jon Tickle, English television host
- May 10
  - Liu Fang, Chinese pipa player
  - Sylvain Wiltord, French footballer
- May 16
  - Laura Pausini, Italian singer
  - Adam Richman, American actor and television personality
- May 17 – Andrea Corr, Irish singer
- May 20
  - Colette Wong, Singaporean sports anchor
  - Mikael Stanne, Swedish singer
- May 23 – Jewel, American singer
- May 26 – Lars Frölander, Swedish swimmer
- May 28 – Misbah-ul-Haq, Pakistani cricketer
- May 29 – Steve Cardenas, American martial artist and retired actor
- May 30
  - Big L, American rapper (d. 1999)
  - CeeLo Green, American singer-songwriter
- May 31 – Kenan Doğulu, Turkish pop musician

June

Bear Grylls

Derek Jeter

- June 1 – Alanis Morissette, Canadian-American singer
- June 2 – Gata Kamsky, American chess player
- June 3 – Martín Karpan, Argentinian actor
- June 7
  - Mahesh Bhupathi, Indian tennis player
  - Bear Grylls, British survivalist
- June 9 – Samoth, Norwegian musician
- June 13
  - Katharina Bellowitsch, Austrian radio and TV presenter.
  - Selma, Icelandic singer, Eurovision Song Contest 1999 runner-up
  - Steve-O, American actor
  - Takahiro Sakurai, Japanese voice actor
- June 22
  - Jo Cox, British Labour Party politician (d.2016)
  - Donald Faison, American actor
- June 23 – Joel Edgerton, Australian actor
- June 25 – Karisma Kapoor, Indian actress
- June 26
  - Jason Craig, American artist
  - Derek Jeter, American baseball player
  - Nicole Saba, Lebanese singer and actress
- June 27 – Christopher O'Neill, British-American businessman; husband of Princess Madeleine of Sweden
- June 28 – Rob Dyrdek, American skateboarder

July

Jeremy Enigk

Jeanna Friske

Josh Radnor

Hilary Swank

- July 1 – Jefferson Pérez, Ecuadorean race walker
- July 2 – Rocky Gray, American musician
- July 7 – Jennifer Jones, Canadian Olympic curling champion
- July 8
  - Dragoslav Jevrić, Montenegrin footballer
  - Jeanna Friske, Russian singer, actress, model and socialite (d. 2015)
- July 12
  - Sharon den Adel, Dutch singer
  - Gregory Helms, American professional wrestler
- July 14
  - David Mitchell, British comedian and actor
  - Martina Hill, German actress, comedian and impersonator
- July 16 – Jeremy Enigk, American singer/songwriter
- July 21 – Terry Coldwell, English singer (East 17)
- July 22 – Franka Potente, German actress
- July 23
  - Kathryn Hahn, American actress
  - Maurice Greene, American athlete
  - Stephanie March, American actress
  - Rik Verbrugghe, Belgian professional road racing cyclist
- July 25 – Lauren Faust, American cartoonist
- July 26 – Daniel Negreanu, Canadian poker player
- July 28 – Alexis Tsipras, Greek politician
- July 29 – Josh Radnor, American actor
- July 30 – Hilary Swank, American actress
- July 31 – Emilia Fox, English actress

August

Amy Adams

Ray Park

Michael Shannon

Derek Fisher

- August 5 – Kajol, a Bollywood actress
- August 7 – Michael Shannon, American actor
- August 8 – Brian Harvey, English singer (East 17)
- August 9 – Derek Fisher, American basketball player
- August 12 – Karl Stefanovic, Australian TV host
- August 13 – Niklas Sundin, Swedish musician
- August 14 – Christopher Gorham, American actor
- August 15 – Natasha Henstridge, Canadian actress and model
- August 16
    - Didier Cuche, Swiss alpine skier
    - Krisztina Egerszegi, Hungarian Olympic champion swimmer
- August 20
    - Amy Adams, American actress
    - Misha Collins, American actor
    - Maxim Vengerov, Russian violinist
- August 22
    - Jenna Leigh Green, American actress and singer
    - Lee Sheppard, Australian cartoonist
- August 23
    - Ray Park, Scottish actor, martial artist
    - Ovi, Romanian-Norwegian singer-songwriter, producer and musician
    - Shifty Shellshock, American singer (Crazy Town)
- August 24 – Jennifer Lien, American actress
- August 28 – Carsten Jancker, German soccer player

September

Jimmy Fallon

Joo Jin-mo

- September 4 – Carmit Bachar, American singer
- September 6
  - Tim Henman, English tennis player
  - Nina Persson, Swedish singer
- September 7 – Glenn Ljungström, Swedish guitarist
- September 10
  - Mirko Filipović, Croatian kickboxer; mixed martial arts fighter
  - Kerry Harvick, American singer
  - Ryan Phillippe, American actor
  - Ben Wallace, American basketball player
- September 12 – Jennifer Nettles, American country music artist (Sugarland)
- September 14 – Hicham El Guerrouj, Moroccan athlete
- September 15 – Wael Kfoury, Lebanese singer, musician, and songwriter
- September 17 – Rasheed Wallace, American basketball player
-

- September 18
  - Sol Campbell, English footballer
  - Xzibit, American rapper
- September 19
  - Jimmy Fallon, American actor, comedian, and television personality; currently hosts The Tonight Show Starring Jimmy Fallon
  - Victoria Silvstedt, Swedish model
- September 23 – Matt Hardy, American professional wrestler
- September 24
  - Niels Brinck, Danish singer and songwriter
  - Kati Wolf, Hungarian singer
- September 26
  - Gary Hall, Jr., American swimmer
  - Joo Jin-mo, South Korean actor
- September 30 – Yul Bürkle, Venezuelan actor and model

October

Charlotte Perrelli

Paul Kariya

Joaquin Phoenix

- October 1 – Keith Duffy, Irish singer (Boyzone)
- October 3 – Marianne Timmer, Dutch speed skater
- October 6 – Hoang Xuan Vinh, Vietnamese shooter
- October 7
  - Allison Munn, American actress
  - Charlotte Perrelli, Swedish singer and occasional television host, Eurovision Song Contest 1999 winner
- October 8 – Koji Murofushi, Japanese hammer thrower
- October 10
  - Dale Earnhardt, Jr., American race car driver
  - Chris Pronger, Canadian hockey player
- October 11 – Jason Arnott, Canadian hockey player
- October 15 – Shumon Basar, British writer and editor
- October 16
  - Aurela Gaçe, Award-winning Albanian singer
  - Paul Kariya, Canadian hockey player
- October 17 – Matthew Macfadyen, English actor
- October 18
  - Jeremy Scahill, writer and documentary film maker
  - Zhou Xun, Chinese actress and singer
- October 20 – Bashar Rahal, American actor
- October 21 – Lera Auerbach, Russian composer and pianist
- October 23
  - Aravind Adiga, Indian-Australian author
  - Sander Westerveld, Dutch soccer player

- October 24 – Catherine Sutherland, Australian actress
- October 28
    - Nelly Ciobanu, Moldovan singer
    - Joaquin Phoenix, Puerto Rican actor
- October 29
    - Akashdeep Saigal, Indian television actor and model
    - Yenny Wahid, a political activist and Islamic Indonesia
- October 31 – Natasja Saad, Danish rapper and reggae singer (d. 2007)

November

Ryan Adams

Leonardo DiCaprio

Stephen Merchant

- November 2 – Nelly, American rapper
- November 4
  - Cedric Bixler-Zavala, Mexican-American singer/lyricist
  - Louise Nurding, English singer
- November 5
  - Ryan Adams, American singer and songwriter
  - Jerry Stackhouse, American basketball player
- November 8
  - Penelope Heyns, South African swimmer
  - Masashi Kishimoto, Japanese manga author
  - Matthew Rhys, Welsh actor
- November 9
  - Alessandro Del Piero, Italian football player
  - Manav Gohil, Indian television actor
- November 11 – Leonardo DiCaprio, American actor
- November 13 – Kerim Seiler, Swiss artist and architect
- November 15 – Chad Kroeger, Canadian singer
- November 16 – Paul Scholes, English football player
- November 18 – Petter Solberg, Norwegian rally driver
- November 20 – Kurt Krömer, German television presenter, comedian and actor
- November 24 – Stephen Merchant, English comedian and actor
- November 27
  - Wendy Houvenaghel, British racing cyclist
  - Zsófia Polgár, Hungarian-born chess player
- November 29 – Ferenc Merkli, Hungarian Slovene priest, writer, translator
- November 30 – Wallace Chung, Hong Kong actor and singer

December

Ryan Seacrest

Rey Mysterio

- December 1 – Costinha, Portuguese footballer
- December 4 – Tadahito Iguchi, Japanese baseball player
- December 7 – Nicole Appleton, Canadian singer (All Saints)
- December 9 – Luisa Bradshaw-White, English actress
- December 10 – Meg White, American rock drummer
- December 11
  - Rey Mysterio, American wrestler
  - Gete Wami, Ethiopian long-distance runner
- December 12 – Michelle Saram, Chindian Singaporean singer and actress
- December 13 – Nick McCarthy, English rock guitarist
- December 17 – Giovanni Ribisi, American actor
- December 18
  - Kari Byron, American artist and television personality
  - Viki Miljković, Serbian singer
  -

- December 19
  - Eduard Ivakdalam, Indonesian footballer
  - Ricky Ponting, Australian cricketer
- December 24
  - Marcelo Salas, Chilean footballer
  - Ryan Seacrest, American television personality
- December 27
  - Fumiko Orikasa, Japanese voice actress and singer
  - Alena Vinnitskaya, Ukrainian singer (Nu Virgos)
- December 29 – Mekhi Phifer, American actor
- December 31 – Tony Kanaan, Brazilian racing driver

Date unknown

- James Singer, American writer

Deaths

January

Glenn Morris

- January 1 – Jimmy Smith, American Major League Baseball infielder (b. 1895)
- January 2 – Tex Ritter, American country musician and actor (b. 1905)
- January 3 – Red Snapp, American baseball player (b. 1888)
- January 5 – Dewey Mayhew, American football coach (b. 1898)

- January 6 – Lech Pijanowski, Polish screenwriter, film critic, broadcaster, and director (b. 1928)
- January 7 – Wang Shusheng, Chinese general (b. 1905)
- January 8 – Charles-Édouard Ferland, Canadian jurist, Liberal politician, and Senator (b. 1892)
- January 10 – Charles G. Bond, U. S. House of Representatives from New York (b. 1877)
- January 11 – Antonio Bautista, Filipino pilot with the Philippine Air Force (b. 1937)
- January 12 – Jack Jacobs, American-born National Football League and Canadian Football League player (b. 1919)
- January 14 – Joseph Dippolito, Italian American Mafia member of the Los Angeles crime syndicate (b. 1914)
- January 15 – Harold D. Cooley, U.S. House of Representatives (b. 1897)
- January 17 – Clara Edwards, American singer, pianist, and composer (b. 1880)
- January 18 – Bill Finger, American comic strip and book writer (b. 1914)
- January 20 – Leonard Freeman, American actor *Hawaii Five-0* (b. 1920)
- January 22 – Oskar Herman, Croatian Jewish painter (b. 1886)
- January 25 – William Fawcett, American character actor, mostly in B-movies (b. 1884)
- January 26 – Julius Patzak, Austrian tenor (b. 1898)
- January 27
  - Georgios Grivas, Greek-Cypriot colonel (b. 1898)
  - Leo Geyr von Schweppenburg, German general (b. 1886)
- January 28 – Oswald Cornwallis, English cricketer (b. 1894)
- January 29 – H. E. Bates, English writer and author (b. 1905)
- January 31
  - Samuel Goldwyn, Polish-born American film studio executive (b. 1879)
  - Einar Texas Ljungberg, Swedish Socialist politician (b. 1880)
  - Glenn Morris, American Olympic decathlete and actor (b. 1912)

February

Satyendra Nath Bose

George Van Biesbroeck

- February 2 – Imre Lakatos, Hungarian philosopher (b. 1922)
- February 3 – Juan de Orduña, Spanish director *Pequeñeces* (1950) (b. 1900)
- February 4 – Satyendra Nath Bose, Indian mathematician and physicist (b. 1894)
- February 5 – Manuel dos Reis Machado, Brazilian martial arts Master (b. 1899)
- February 7 – Edward Beck (British Army officer), British Army (b. 1880)
- February 8 – Fritz Zwicky, Swiss astronomer (b. 1898)
- February 9 – Raymond A. Wheeler, Lieutenant-General United States Armed Forces (b. 1885)

- February 11 – Ghantasala (singer), Indian playback singer and music composer (b. 1922)
- February 15
  - Kurt Atterberg, Swedish composer (b. 1887)
  - George W. Snedecor, American mathematician and statistician (b. 1881)
- February 16 – Horace Kallen, American philosopher.(b. 1882)
- February 17 – Ralph W. Gerard, American neurophysiologist and behavioural scientist (b. 1900)
- February 18 – Duncan Archibald Graham, Canadian physician (b. 1882)
- February 21 – Tim Horton, Canadian hockey defenseman with Toronto Maple Leafs, New York Rangers, Pittsburgh Penguins, and Buffalo Sabres. Co-Founder of the Tim Hortons restaurant chain. (b. 1930)
- February 22 – Samuel Byck, American airplane hijacker and murderer (b. 1930)
- February 23
  - William F. Knowland, American politician and newspaper owner (b. 1908)
  - George Van Biesbroeck, Belgian-American astronomer (b. 1880)
- February 24
  - Margaret Leech, American historian and fiction writer (b. 1893)
  - Robert A. Stemmle, German screenwriter and film director (b. 1903)
- February 27 – Princess Nina Georgievna of Russia, Russian great-granddaughter of Tsar Nicholas I of Russia (b. 1901)
- February 28 – Carole Lesley, British actress (b. 1935)

March

- March 1
  - Hüseyin Kemal Gürmen, Turkish theatre and cinema actor (b. 1901)

- o Bobby Timmons, American jazz pianist and composer (b. 1935)
- March 2 – Péter Schell, Hungarian politician (b. 1898)
- March 3
  - o Barbara Ruick, American actress and singer (b. 1930)
  - o Frank Wilcox, American character actor (b. 1907)
- March 4 – Adolph Gottlieb, American abstract expressionist painter (b. 1903)
- March 5
  - o John Samuel Bourque, French-Canadian politician, Cabinet Minister, military member, and businessman from Québec, Canada (b. 1894)
  - o Billy De Wolfe, American character actor (b. 1907)
- March 6 – Ernest Becker, American anthropologist and writer; who won the 1974 Pulitzer Prize (posthumously) for his book *The Denial of Death* (b. 1924)
- March 7
  - o Moriji Mochida, last person ever awarded the 10th dan rank in kendo (b. 1885)
  - o Hans Sachs, Holocaust survivor and poster collector (b. 1881)
- March 8 – Martha Wentworth, American actress (b. 1889)
- March 9 – Earl Wilbur Sutherland Jr., American physiologist, Nobel Prize laureate (b. 1915)
- March 10 – Alexander John Majeski, American architect and former Naval Lieutenant (b. 1920)
- March 12 – Oleksii Shovkunenko, Ukrainian painter (b. 1884)
- March 17 – Louis Kahn, Estonian architect (b. 1901)
- March 19 – Edward Platt, American actor known as, "The Chief" on NBC/CBS's *Get Smart* (b. 1916)
- March 20 – Chet Huntley, American television reportor (b. 1911)
- March 21 – Candy Darling, American actress (b. 1944)
- March 22 – Peter Revson, American race car driver (b. 1939)
- March 24 – Lewie G. Merritt, U. S. Marine, major general and aviator (b. 1897)

- March 27 – Wilhelm Herget, German Luftwaffe flying ace (b. 1910)
- March 29
    - Andrea Checchi, Italian actor (*La ciociara*) (b. 1916)
    - Joe Stecher, American professional wrestler (b. 1893)
- March 31 – Frank Seno, American football running back and defensive back (b. 1921)

April

Georges Pompidou

Ayub Khan

Franz Jonas

Agnes Moorehead

- April 2
  - Douglass Dumbrille, Pioneering Canadian actor in Hollywood (b. 1889)
  - Georges Pompidou, President of France (b. 1911)
- April 3 – Ossie Newton-Thompson, South African cricketer and politician (b. 1920)
- April 5 – A. Y. Jackson, Canadian painter and a founding member of the Group of Seven (b. 1882)
- April 6
  - Willem Marinus Dudok, Dutch modernist architect (b. 1884)
  - Roy Wood, American professional baseball player (b. 1892)
- April 8 – K. A. C. Creswell, English architectural historian (b. 1879)
- April 11 – Edward Alexander Bott, psychologist at the University of Toronto (b. 1887)
- April 14 – Howard Pease, American adventure novelist (b. 1894)
- April 18
  - Betty Compson, American actress (b. 1897)
  - Marcel Pagnol, French novelist (b. 1895)
- April 19 – Ayub Khan, President of Pakistan (b. 1907)
- April 20 – Peter Lee Lawrence, German actor in Spaghetti Westerns; such as (*For a Few Dollars More*) (b. 1944)
- April 21 – Mirja Mane, Finnish actress (b. 1929)
- April 23 – Cy Williams, American baseball player (b. 1887)
- April 24
  - Bud Abbott, American comedian (b. 1895)
  - Franz Jonas, 7th President of Austria (b. 1899)

- April 27 – Hans W. Petersen, Danish actor of over 40 films (b. 1897)
- April 28 – Paul Page, American actor of the 1920s and 1930s (b. 1903)
- April 30 – Agnes Moorehead, American actress (b. 1900)

May

Duke Ellington

- May 1 – Frank Packer, Australian media proprietor (b. 1906)
- May 2
  - James O. Richardson, American admiral (b. 1878)
  - William Wantling, American ex-Marine, poet, and novelist (b. 1933)
- May 3 – Ralph McCabe, Canadian-born Major League Baseball player (b. 1918)
- May 4 – Ludwig Karl Koch, German-born broadcaster and sound recordist in the United Kingdom (b. 1881)
- May 6 – Robert Maestri, American of Italian heritage who served as mayor of New Orleans from (1936 to 1946) (b. 1889)
- May 7 – Abu Bakar of Pahang, Fourth Sultan of Pahang (b. 1904)
- May 8 – Fred Conyngham, Australian actor (b. 1901)
- May 10 – Takeshi Sakamoto, Japanese versatile actor (b. 1899)
- May 12 – Wayne Maki, Canadian National Hockey League player with Chicago, St. Louis, and Vancouver; (died of brain cancer) (b. 1944)

- May 14 – Jacob L. Moreno, Austrian-American leading psychiatrist and psychosociologist (b. 1889)
- May 15 – Guy Simonds, English-born, Canadian Lieutenant-General who commanded the Canadian Armed Forces in World War II (b. 1903)
- May 16 – Billy Welu, American profession bowler (b. 1932)
- May 17 – Symbionese Liberation Army Los Angeles police shootout of its members
  - Angela Atwood, American founding member of the Symbionese Liberation Army (b. 1949)
  - Donald DeFreeze, American leader of the Symbionese Liberation Army; who went by the nom de guerre "Field Marshall Cinque" (b. 1943)
  - Camilla Hall, American member of the Symbionese Liberation Army; one of main kidnappers of heiress Patricia Hearst (b. 1945)
  - Nancy Ling Perry, An American member of the Symbionese Liberation Army (b. 1947)
  - Patricia Soltysik, American member of the Symbionese Liberation Army (b. 1950)
- May 18 – Harry Ricardo, broadcaster and sound recordist (b. 1881)
- May 19 – Allal al-Fassi, Moroccan politician, poet, writer, and scholar (b. 1910)
- May 21 – Lily Kronberger, Hungarian figure skater (b. 1890)
- May 24 – Duke Ellington, American jazz pianist and bandleader (b. 1899)
- May 25
  - Donald Crisp, English-American actor (b. 1882)
  - Arturo Jauretche, Argentine writer, politician, and philosopher (b. 1901)
- May 26 – Kitty Gordon, English stage and silent film actress. (b. 1878)
- May 27 – Rudolf Altstadt, German soldier in World War II (b. 1914)
- May 28 – Francesco Fausto Nitti, Italian journalist (b. 1899)
-

- May 31
  - Adelle Davis, American author and nutritionist (b. 1904)
  - Frederick George Topham, Canadian soldier and recipient of the Victoria Cross (b. 1917)

June

- June 1 – Henry Clay Sevier, American lawyer and member from Louisiana House of Representatives (b. 1896)
- June 2 – Roger C. Slaughter, American lawyer and U. S. Representative from Missouri (b. 1905)
- June 3 – Rashid Nezhmetdinov, Soviet chess player (b. 1912)
- June 4
  - Smokey Harris, Canadian ice hockey player (b. 1890)
  - Mamerto Urriolagoitía, President of Bolivia from 1949 to 1951 (b. 1895)
- June 5 – Larry Cabrelli, American football player and assistant coach Philadelphia Eagles (b. 1917)
- June 7 – Abdul Rahman Hashim, Malaysian Inspector-General of Police (b. 1925)
- June 9
  - Miguel Ángel Asturias, Guatemalan writer, Nobel Prize laureate (b. 1890)
  - Katharine Cornell, Berlin-born, American stage actress, writer, theatre owner, and producer (b. 1893)
- June 10 – Prince Henry, Duke of Gloucester, Governor-General of Australia (b. 1900)
- June 11
  - Julius Evola, Italian philosopher (b. 1898)
  - Eurico Gaspar Dutra, Brazilian marshal and 16th President of Brazil (b. 1883)
- June 12 – André Marie, French Radical politician (b. 1897)
- June 14 – Knud Jeppesen, Danish musicologist, composer, and songwriter (b. 1892)
- June 15 – Kevin Gately, English mathematics student at University of Warwick involved in the Red Lion Square disorders (b. 1953)

- June 16 – Mauritz Hugo, Swedish-born, American film and television actor (b. 1909)
- June 17 – Austin Gunsel, 3rd commissioner of the National Football League (b. 1909)
- June 18 – Georgy Zhukov, Soviet general (World War II) (b. 1896)
- June 21 – Katsutaro Kouta, Japanese female geisha and ryūkōka singer (b. 1904)
- June 22 – Darius Milhaud, French composer (b. 1892)
- June 23 – Calvin B. Hoover, noted U. S. economist and professor (b. 1897)
- June 24 – József Juhász, Hungarian stage and film actor (b. 1908)
- June 25 – Cornelius Lanczos, Hungarian mathematician and physicist (b. 1893)
- June 26 – Ernest Gruening, American journalist, Governor of Alaska Territory from 1939 to 1953, and United States Senator from 1959 to 1969 (b. 1887)
- June 27 – Fred DeStefano, American football player and physician; who won the National Football League title with the Chicago Cardinals of 1925 (b. 1900)
- June 28
  - Vannevar Bush, American engineer, inventor and science administrator (b. 1890)
  - Frank Sutton, American actor (b. 1923)
- June 30 – Alberta Williams King, American civil rights champion, wife of Martin Luther King, Sr., and mother of Martin Luther King, Jr. (Shot) (b. 1904)

July

Juan Domingo Perón

James Chadwick

Erich Kästner

- July 1 – Juan Domingo Perón, President of Argentina (b. 1895)
- July 2
  - ○ Sonia Holm, English actress (b. 1920)
  - ○ Edith L. Sharp, Canadian writer (b. 1911)
- July 4 – Georgette Heyer, British writer (b. 1902)
- July 6 – Joseph Baldacchino, Maltese archaeologist (b. 1894)
- July 7
  - ○ Leon Shamroy, American Academy Award-winning cinematographer (b. 1901)
  - ○ Cornelius Vanderbilt IV, American publisher and member of the Vanderbilt Family (b. 1898)
- July 8 – Margaret Furse, English Academy Award-winning costume designer for *Anne of the Thousand Days* (b. 1911)
- July 9 – Earl Warren, Governor of California and Chief Justice of the United States Supreme Court (b. 1891)
- July 10 – Nancy Wickwire, American soap opera actress (b. 1925)
- July 11 – Pär Lagerkvist, Swedish writer, Nobel Prize laureate (b. 1891)

- July 12 – Sonja Ludvigsen, Norwegian politician (b. 1928)
- July 13 – Patrick Blackett, English physicist, Nobel Prize laureate (b. 1897)
- July 14
  - Dame Sibyl Hathaway, Seigneur of Sark (b. 1884)
  - Carl Andrew Spaatz, American general (b. 1891)
- July 15
  - William Albrecht, Chairman of the Department of Soils at the University of Missouri (b. 1888)
  - Christine Chubbuck, American TV personality (b. 1944)
  - Victor Negus, British surgeon (b. 1887)
- July 16 – Oduvaldo Vianna Filho, Brazilian playwright (b. 1936)
- July 17 – Dizzy Dean, American baseball player (St. Louis Cardinals) and a member of the MLB Hall of Fame (b. 1910)
- July 19 – Joe Flynn, American actor (b. 1924)
- July 20 – Charles Rudolph d'Olive, American World War I ace (b. 1896)
- July 22 – Wayne Morse, American lawyer, politician, and United States Senator from Oregon (1945–1969) (b. 1900)
- July 23 – Peter Lei, Bishop of Hong Kong (b. 1922)
- July 24 – Sir James Chadwick, English physicist, Nobel Prize laureate (b. 1891)
- July 25 – Robert Hanbidge, Canadian lawyer, {municipal, provincial, & federal} politician; including the Mayor of Kerrobert, and 12th Lieutenant-Governor of Saskatchewan (b. 1891)
- July 27
  - Lightnin' Slim, American blues musician (b. 1913)
  - Joop Pelser, Dutch footballer (b. 1892)
- July 28 – Truman Bradley, American radio actor (b. 1905)
- July 29
  - "Mama Cass" Elliot, American vocalist (b. 1941)
  - Erich Kästner, German author (b. 1899)
- July 30 – Lev Knipper, Russian composer (b. 1898)

August

Charles Lindbergh

- August 2 – Cyril Smith, English virtuoso concert pianist (b. 1909)
- August 3
  - Edna Murphy, American actress of the silent era (b. 1899)
  - Almira Sessions, American character actress (b. 1888)
- August 4 – Józef Kondrat, Polish stage and film actor (b. 1902)
- August 5 – Friedrich F. Tippmann, Hungarian entomologist (b. 1894)
- August 6 – Gunboat Smith, Irish-American boxer and referee (b. 1887)
- August 7 – Rosario Castellanos, Méxican poet and author (b. 1925)
- August 8 – Baldur von Schirach, Nazi German Hitler Youth leader (b. 1907)
- August 11
  - José Falcón, Portuguese matador (gored to death by bull) (b. 1944)
  - Jan Tschichold, German-born typographer (b. 1902)
- August 14 – Romuald Bourque, French-Canadian politician from Québec (b. 1889)
- August 15 – Edmund Cobb, American actor whose career spanner nearly 55 years (b. 1892)
- August 17 – Aldo Palazzeschi, Italian novelist, poet, journalist and essayist (b. 1885)
- August 18 – J. C. Winslow, English missionary to India for Society for the Propagation of the Gospel (b. 1882)
- August 19 – Rodger Davies, American diplomat (assassinated) (b. 1921)

- August 20 – Magda Sonja, Austrian actress (b. 1886)
- August 21 – Buford Pusser, American Sheriff of McNairy County, Tennessee (b. 1937)
- August 22 – Jacob Bronowski, Polish-Jewish British mathematician, biologist and science historian (b. 1908)
- August 23 – Roberto Assagioli, Italian psychiatrist and pioneer (b. 1888)
- August 24 – Alexander P. de Seversky, Russian-American aviation pioneer and inventor (b. 1894)
- August 26 – Charles Lindbergh, American aviator (*Spirit of St. Louis*) (b. 1902)
- August 27 – Otto Strasser, Nazi German politician (b. 1897)
- August 28 – Aleksandar Sekulović, Montenegrin cinematographer (b. 1918)
- August 29
  - Judith Furse, English actress (b. 1912)
  - Fred W. Preller, American, New York-based politician (b. 1902)
- August 30 – Kenneth Anderson, Indian-born British writer and hunter (b. 1910)
- August 31 – Gianna Manzini, Italian writer (b. 1896)

September

Mary Broadfoot Walker

- September 1 – Mary Broadfoot Walker, British physician (b. 1888)

- September 2 – Walter Strenge, American cinematographer (b. 1898)
- September 3 – Harry Partch, American composer (b. 1901)
- September 4
  - Creighton Williams Abrams, American general (b. 1914)
  - Marcel Achard, French playwright and scriptwriter (b. 1899)
- September 6
  - Olga Baclanova, Russian stage and screen actress, operatic singer, and ballerina (b. c. 1893)
  - Otto Kruger, American actor of German descent (b. 1885)
- September 7 – Juan Antonio Ipiña, Spanish football manager (b. 1912)
- September 8
  - Bert Niehoff, American Major League Baseball player (b. 1884)
  - Jimmy Swinnerton, American cartoonist, *Little Jimmy* (b. 1875)
- September 10 – Melchior Wańkowicz, Polish army officer, writer, journalist, and publisher (b. 1892)
- September 11 – Robert Nodar, Jr., American Republican politician from New York and its member of the United States House of Representatives (b. 1916)
- September 12 – Craig Woods, American actor (b. 1918)
- September 15 – René Capistrán Garza, Méxican Association of Catholic Youth leader, lawyer, screenwriter, and film critic (b. 1898)
- September 16 – Phog Allen, American basketball and baseball player (b. 1885)
- September 17 – Claudia Morgan, American actress, *The Edge of Night* in the 1950s (b. 1912)
- September 18 – Edna Best, English actress (b. 1900)
- September 19
  - Tránsito Cocomarola, Argentine musician and folklorist (b. 1918)
  - Zack Taylor, American baseball player and manager (b. 1898)

- September 20 – Fray José de Guadalupe Mojica, Mexican Franciscan friar; former tenor and film actor (b. 1896)
- September 21 – Walter Brennan, American actor; 3-time Best Supporting Academy Award-winning actor (1936, 1938, & 1940) (b. 1894)
- September 22
  - Winfried Otto Schumann, German physicist (b. 1888)
  - George Spahn, American rancher connected to the Manson family (b. 1889)
- September 23 – Cliff Arquette, American comedian who created the character *Charlie Weaver* (b. 1905)
- September 26 – Jean Gale, American vaudeville performer (b. 1912)
- September 27
  - Silvio Frondizi, Argentine intellectual and lawyer (b. 1907)
  - James R. Webb, American soldier and screenwriter who won the 1963 Academy Award for *How the West Was Won (film)* (b. 1909)
- September 28 – Arnold Fanck, German film director who pioneered in the mountain film genre (b. 1889)

October

Ed Sullivan

- October 1
  - Frederick Moosbrugger, American admiral (b. 1900)
  - Stephen Latchford, American diplomat and aviation expert (b. 1883)

- October 2 – Vasily Shukshin, Soviet/Russian actor, writer, screenwriter, and director from the Altai region (b. 1929)
- October 3 – Bessie Louise Pierce, American historian (b. 1888)
- October 4
  - Robert Lee Moore, American mathematician (b. 1882)
  - Anne Sexton, American poet and writer (b. 1928)
- October 5 – Virgil Miller, American cinematographer (b. 1886)
- October 6 – V. K. Krishna Menon, Indian statesman, diplomat, and nationalist (b. 1896)
- October 7 – Henry J. Cadbury, American biblical scholar and Quaker (b. 1883)
- October 8 – Harry Carney, American jazz musician (b. 1910)
- October 9
  - Theodore Foley, American Catholic priest (b. 1913)
  - Oskar Schindler, Sudetgerman businessman (b. 1908)
- October 10 – Werner Heyking, Danish actor, *Willy Wonka & the Chocolate Factory* (1971) (b. 1913)
- October 11 – Frank Kowalski, American soldier United States Army and United States Representatives from Connecticut (b. 1907)
- October 13
  - Sam Rice, American baseball player (Washington Senators) and a member of the MLB Hall of Fame (b. 1890)
  - Ed Sullivan, American television host (b. 1901)
- October 14 – Sattar Bahlulzade, Azerbaijani landscape painter (b. 1909)
- October 17 – Tomotaka Tasaka, Japanese film director (b. 1902)
- October 18 – Anders Lange, Norwegian politician (b. 1902)
- October 19
  - Farrukh Ahmad, Bangladeshi poet and writer (b. 1918)
  - Nur Ali Elahi, Iranian jurist, musician, and spiritual thinker (b. 1895)
- October 20 – Élie Lescot, former President of Haiti (b. 1883)
- October 21 – Donald Goines, American witer of urban fiction (b. 1936)

- October 23 – Melchior Lengyel, Hungarian writer, dramatist, and film screenwriter (b. 1880)
- October 24 – David Oistrakh, Ukrainian violinist (b. 1908)
- October 25 – Fahrettin Altay, Ottoman military officer (b. 1880)
- October 26 – Bidia Dandaron, Buryat Buddhist practitioner in the USSR (b. 1914)
- October 27
    - Paul Frankeur, French actor (b. 1905)
    - C. P. Ramanujam, Indian mathematician (b. 1938)
- October 30 – Begum Akhtar, Indian singer (b. 1914)
- October 31 – Mikheil Chiaureli, Soviet Georgian filmmaker (b. 1894)

November

U Thant

- November 1 – Ralf Harolde, American character actor (b, 1899)
- November 2
    - Richard Kroner, German neo-Hegelian philosopher (b. 1884)
    - Farid-ud-Din Qadri, Pakistani Islamic scholar (b. c. 1918)
- November 3 – Mamá Tingó, Dominican activist (b. 1921)
- November 4 – Harry Fritz, American baseball player Chicago Whales (b. 1890)
- November 5
    - Marguerite Namara, American lyric soprano (b. 1888)
    - Stafford Repp, American actor noted for his work on the *Batman (TV Series)* (b. 1918)
- November 7 – Eric Linklater, British author (b. 1899)

- November 8 – Ivory Joe Hunter, American rhythm & blues singer, songwriter, and pianist (b. 1914)
- November 9 – Egon Wellesz, British composer, teacher and musicologist (b. 1885)
- November 10 – Jasper Goodwill, American municipal politician, Mayor of Minden, Louisiana (b. 1889)
- November 13
  - Vittorio De Sica, Italian actor and film director (b. 1901)
  - Karen Silkwood, American chemical technician and labour union activist (b. 1946)
- November 14 – Johnny Mack Brown, American football star and actor (b. 1904)
- November 15 – Konstantin Shayne, Russian-born, American actor (b. 1888)
- November 16 – Walther Meissner, German technical physicist (b. 1882)
- November 17 – Erskine Hamilton Childers, 4th President of Ireland (b. 1905)
- November 18 – Gösta Lilliehöök, Swedish pentathlete and 1912 Olympic Games champion (b. 1884)
- November 19 – Alessandro Momo, Italian actor (b. 1956)
- November 21 – Frank Martin, Swiss composer (b. 1890)
- November 23
  - Cornelius Ryan, Irish-American writer (b. 1920)
  - Massacre of the Sixty in Ethiopia of government and military officials.
    - Abiye Abebe, politician and army officer (b. 1918)
    - Aklilu Habte-Wold, politician and Prime Minister of Ethiopia (b. 1912)
    - Aman Andom, army officer and Chairman of the Derg (b. 1924)
    - Asrate Medhin Kassa, aristocrat and army officer (b. 1922)
    - Endelkachew Makonnen, politician and Prime Minister of Ethiopia (b. 1927)
    -

- November 25
    - Nick Drake, British musician (b. 1948)
    - U Thant, Burmese diplomat and Secretary-General of the United Nations (b. 1909)
- November 27 – T. A. Madhuram, Tamil stage & film actress and film producer (b. 1918)
- November 28 – Konstantin Melnikov, Soviet architect (b. 1890)
- November 29
    - James J. Braddock, American boxer (b. 1905)
    - Peng Dehuai, Chinese leader (b. 1898)

December

Richard Long

Zachary Cope

- December 2
    - Sophie Carmen Eckhardt-Gramatté, Russian-born, Canadian composer, virtuoso pianist, & violinist (b. 1899)

- o Max Weber, Swiss Federal Councilor (b. 1897)
- December 3 – Hans Leibelt, German film actor (b. 1885)
- December 4 – Lee Kinsolving, American actor (b. 1938)
- December 5
  - o Pietro Germi, Italian film director (b. 1914)
  - o Zaharia Stancu, Romanian prose writer (b. 1902)
- December 6
  - o Frederik Jacobus Johannes Buytendijk, Dutch anthropologist, biologist and psychologist (b. 1887)
  - o Nikolay Gerasimovich Kuznetsov, Soviet admiral (b. 1904)
  - o Luigi Salvatorelli, Italian historian and publicist (b. 1886)
- December 7 – Ariyavangsagatayana, 17th Supreme Patriarch of Thailand, Member of the Chetupon Temple (b. 1896)
- December 8 – Nadia Benois, Russian painter and stage designer; also the mother of English actor Peter Ustinov (b. 1896)
- December 9
  - o Hans Traut, German General-Lieutenant in the Nazi Wehrmacht in World War II (b. 1895)
  - o Ludwig Weber, Austrian bass (b. 1899)
- December 10 – Paul Richards, American actor, *Beneath the Planet of the Apes* (b. 1924)
- December 11 – Reed Hadley, American radio, television, & film actor (b. 1911)
- December 12 – Booker McDaniels, American baseball pitcher in the Negro Leagues with (Kansas City Monarchs) (b. 1913)
- December 13 – John G. Bennett, British mathematician (b. 1897)
- December 14 – Walter Lippmann, American writer and journalist (b. 1889)
- December 15 – Anatole Litvak, Ukrainian-born film director (b. 1902)
- December 16 – Kostas Varnalis, Greek poet (b. 1884)
- December 17 – Bing Slamet, Indonesian singer, songwriter, comedian and actor (b. 1927)
- December 18 – Harry Hooper, American baseball player (Boston Red Sox) and a member of the MLB Hall of Fame (b. 1887)
- December 19

- o Bernd von Brauchitsch, German air force officer (b. 1911)
- o Catrano Catrani, Italian-Argentine director & producer (b. 1910)
- December 20 – André Jolivet, French composer (b. 1905)
- December 21 – Richard Long, American actor (b. 1927)
- December 22 – Gordon Purdy, Canadian Liberal politician (b. 1888)
- December 23 – Jules Rykovich, Croatian-born, American football player (b. 1923)
- December 24 – Sentarō Ōmori, Japanese admiral (b. 1892)
- December 25 – Gorman Kennedy, Canadian executive and general manager of the Montréal Alouettes from (1957 to 1959) (b. c. 1907 or 1908)
- December 26 – Jack Benny, American comedian (b. 1894)
- December 27
  - o Bob Custer, American film actor (b. 1898)
  - o Vladimir Fock, Soviet physicist (b. 1898)
  - o Ned Maddrell, last surviving native speaker of the Manx language (b. 1877)
- December 28 – Zachary Cope, English physician and surgeon (b. 1881)
- December 29 – William Charles Fuller, Welsh soldier and recipient of the Victoria Cross (b. 1884
- December 30
  - o George Howard Earle III, American politician and diplomat; served as Governor of Pennsylvania from 1935–1939 (b. 1890)
  - o Sid Terris, American boxer (b. 1904)
- December 31
  - o Dogen Handa, Japanese professional Go player (b. 1914)
  - o Robert Pache, Swiss footballer (b. 1897)

Nobel Prizes

- Physics – Sir Martin Ryle, Antony Hewish
- Chemistry – Paul J. Flory
- Medicine – Albert Claude, Christian de Duve, George E. Palade
- Literature – Eyvind Johnson, Harry Martinson
- Peace – Seán MacBride, Eisaku Satō
- Economics – Gunnar Myrdal, Friedrich Hayek

In the News

IRA begins bombing campaign on mainland Britain and bombs The Tower of London on July 17th and the Houses of parliament and pubs in Birmingham.

Following impeachment hearings started on May 9th Richard Nixon becomes the first US president forced to resign after the Watergate Scandal on August 9th.

On October 30th, 1974 the much hyped boxing match between George Foreman and Muhammad Ali for Ali to regain his heavyweight title takes place in Kinshasa, Zaire (Democratic Republic of the Congo).

55 MPH Speed Limit imposed to preserve gas usage US wide.

Sears Tower in Chicago becomes the worlds tallest building.

President Ford announces an amnesty program for Vietnam War deserters and draft evaders.

Stephen King publishes his debut novel, Carrie,

Estimate of The Worlds Population reaches 4 billion.

The French President Georges Pompidou dies while in Office.

West Germany Wins 1974 World Cup in West Germany.

Pocket calculators start to appear in shops.

Popular Films,- The Sting, The Exorcist, Papillon, Herbie Rides Again.

1974 Calendar

January 1974
Sun	Mon	Tue	Wed	Thu	Fri	Sat
		1	2	3	4	5
6	7	8	9	10	11	12
13	14	15	16	17	18	19
20	21	22	23	24	25	26
27	28	29	30	31		

February 1974
Sun	Mon	Tue	Wed	Thu	Fri	Sat
					1	2
3	4	5	6	7	8	9
10	11	12	13	14	15	16
17	18	19	20	21	22	23
24	25	26	27	28		

March 1974
Sun	Mon	Tue	Wed	Thu	Fri	Sat
					1	2
3	4	5	6	7	8	9
10	11	12	13	14	15	16
17	18	19	20	21	22	23
24	25	26	27	28	29	30
31						

April 1974
Sun	Mon	Tue	Wed	Thu	Fri	Sat
	1	2	3	4	5	6
7	8	9	10	11	12	13
14	15	16	17	18	19	20
21	22	23	24	25	26	27
28	29	30				

May 1974
Sun	Mon	Tue	Wed	Thu	Fri	Sat
			1	2	3	4
5	6	7	8	9	10	11
12	13	14	15	16	17	18
19	20	21	22	23	24	25
26	27	28	29	30	31	

June 1974
Sun	Mon	Tue	Wed	Thu	Fri	Sat
						1
2	3	4	5	6	7	8
9	10	11	12	13	14	15
16	17	18	19	20	21	22
23	24	25	26	27	28	29
30						

July 1974
Sun	Mon	Tue	Wed	Thu	Fri	Sat
	1	2	3	4	5	6
7	8	9	10	11	12	13
14	15	16	17	18	19	20
21	22	23	24	25	26	27
28	29	30	31			

August 1974
Sun	Mon	Tue	Wed	Thu	Fri	Sat
				1	2	3
4	5	6	7	8	9	10
11	12	13	14	15	16	17
18	19	20	21	22	23	24
25	26	27	28	29	30	31

September 1974
Sun	Mon	Tue	Wed	Thu	Fri	Sat
1	2	3	4	5	6	7
8	9	10	11	12	13	14
15	16	17	18	19	20	21
22	23	24	25	26	27	28
29	30					

October 1974
Sun	Mon	Tue	Wed	Thu	Fri	Sat
		1	2	3	4	5
6	7	8	9	10	11	12
13	14	15	16	17	18	19
20	21	22	23	24	25	26
27	28	29	30	31		

November 1974
Sun	Mon	Tue	Wed	Thu	Fri	Sat
					1	2
3	4	5	6	7	8	9
10	11	12	13	14	15	16
17	18	19	20	21	22	23
24	25	26	27	28	29	30

December 1974
Sun	Mon	Tue	Wed	Thu	Fri	Sat
1	2	3	4	5	6	7
8	9	10	11	12	13	14
15	16	17	18	19	20	21
22	23	24	25	26	27	28
29	30	31